THE STORY OF

MARTHA STEWART

LIVING®

ELIZABETH SIRIMARCO

SMART APPLE MEDIA MANKATO MINNESOTA

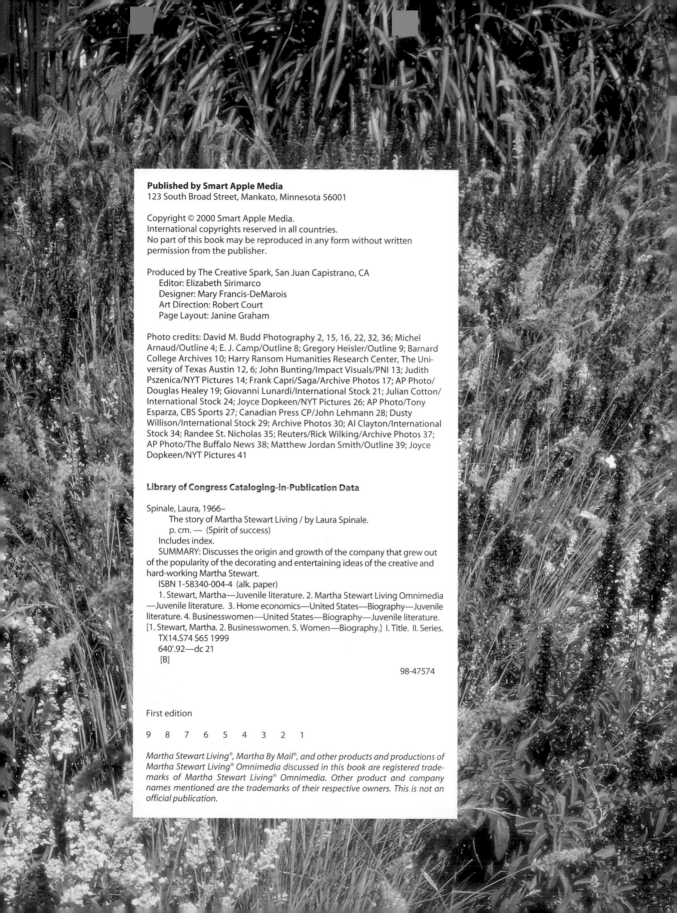

Published by Smart Apple Media
123 South Broad Street, Mankato, Minnesota 56001

Copyright © 2000 Smart Apple Media.
International copyrights reserved in all countries.
No part of this book may be reproduced in any form without written
permission from the publisher.

Produced by The Creative Spark, San Juan Capistrano, CA
Editor: Elizabeth Sirimarco
Designer: Mary Francis-DeMarois
Art Direction: Robert Court
Page Layout: Janine Graham

Photo credits: David M. Budd Photography 2, 15, 16, 22, 32, 36; Michel
Arnaud/Outline 4; E. J. Camp/Outline 8; Gregory Heisler/Outline 9; Barnard
College Archives 10; Harry Ransom Humanities Research Center, The Uni-
versity of Texas Austin 12, 6; John Bunting/Impact Visuals/PNI 13; Judith
Pszenica/NYT Pictures 14; Frank Capri/Saga/Archive Photos 17; AP Photo/
Douglas Healey 19; Giovanni Lunardi/International Stock 21; Julian Cotton/
International Stock 24; Joyce Dopkeen/NYT Pictures 26; AP Photo/Tony
Esparza, CBS Sports 27; Canadian Press CP/John Lehmann 28; Dusty
Willison/International Stock 29; Archive Photos 30; Al Clayton/International
Stock 34; Randee St. Nicholas 35; Reuters/Rick Wilking/Archive Photos 37;
AP Photo/The Buffalo News 38; Matthew Jordan Smith/Outline 39; Joyce
Dopkeen/NYT Pictures 41

Library of Congress Cataloging-in-Publication Data

Spinale, Laura, 1966–
    The story of Martha Stewart Living / by Laura Spinale.
    p. cm. — (Spirit of success)
    Includes index.
    SUMMARY: Discusses the origin and growth of the company that grew out
of the popularity of the decorating and entertaining ideas of the creative and
hard-working Martha Stewart.
    ISBN 1-58340-004-4 (alk. paper)
    1. Stewart, Martha—Juvenile literature. 2. Martha Stewart Living Omnimedia
—Juvenile literature. 3. Home economics—United States—Biography—Juvenile
literature. 4. Businesswomen—United States—Biography—Juvenile literature.
[1. Stewart, Martha. 2. Businesswomen. 5. Women—Biography.] I. Title. II. Series.
    TX14.S74 S65 1999
    640′.92—dc 21
    [B]
                                                                98-47574

First edition

9 8 7 6 5 4 3 2 1

Table of Contents

Mad about Martha

When Martha Kostyra Stewart was growing up in Nutley, New Jersey, her parents didn't have much money. Mr. and Mrs. Kostyra couldn't afford to give any of their six children an allowance, but Martha needed some money. She wanted to buy cloth to sew the stylish clothes she loved, and she wanted to invest in some seeds to plant in the family garden. Martha realized that to pay for the things she wanted, she would have to raise the money herself.

Martha started organizing birthday parties for her friends. She baked their cakes and decorated their living rooms. Her fees varied from party to party, but she always made more than the 50 cents an hour she had charged for baby-sitting.

Today Martha Stewart serves as the chairman and **chief executive officer** of her own company—Martha Stewart Living® **Omnimedia.** (*Omni* is a Latin word meaning "all.") The company publishes books, magazines, and newspaper columns. It also produces the popular television show *Martha Stewart Living* and a radio show called *askMartha*. Martha Stewart Living Omnimedia also sells decorating products at Kmart® and Zellers® and more selections through the Martha By Mail® catalog. The company even operates its own **Internet** site.

No one really knows how much Martha Stewart made organizing parties as a girl, but her company earned approximately $200 million in 1998. While the company is vastly different from the teenage enterprises of Martha Kostyra, its goals and interests remain much the same. Martha Stewart Living Omnimedia helps people who want to make their houses prettier, their gardens more colorful, and their food tastier. The company's main objective is to help its customers create a more appealing **lifestyle** for themselves.

Any company that wants to be successful must find a **niche** and then fill it. In the business world, filling a niche means coming up with an idea for a product or service that a company does well and that has not been offered in the past.

A young cadet escorts Martha to a dance. Martha kept busy as a teenager, working hard at school and organizing special parties for her friends, but she still found time to date and have fun.

Before Martha Stewart came along, no one ever thought of earning millions by selling mix-and-match bed sheets, teaching people how to make their own Christmas wreaths, or showing admiring readers how to garnish their ham with freshly picked grass. No one realized how many people in North America would spend money on books and magazines that teach such skills, or how many television viewers would watch programs to learn how to complete intricate projects step-by-step.

Of course Martha Stewart did not proceed directly from throwing parties for her childhood friends to becoming the chairman and chief executive officer of a multimillion-dollar company. She first had to graduate from high school and college and then prove herself by succeeding at several jobs. Nonetheless, many of the character traits she developed in her youth have helped Martha succeed at virtually every task she undertakes.

What are some of the traits that helped create a superstar businessperson? Martha Stewart is disciplined. As a teenager and young adult, she spent a lot of time studying and usually made excellent grades in high school and college. She is driven, working extremely long hours to achieve her goals. Martha usually sleeps only four hours each night so she has more time to devote to her business. She is a perfectionist, wanting every item produced and sold by her company to be the best it can be. She is creative, constantly dreaming up new products to sell. She also develops new decorating, craft, garden-ing, and cooking ideas for her magazines, books, and television show. Finally, Martha Stewart uses her creativity to think of ways to expand her company.

Martha Stewart enjoys an afternoon at her Connecticut home. Her successful company is the product of many years spent practicing the things she loves to do: cooking, gardening, decorating, and maintaining a beautiful home.

Martha Stewart by the Stats

Martha Stewart's popularity can be measured by the number of projects she has going: her daily television and radio shows, her books, her magazines, her catalog, and her Web site. Still, sometimes it's easier to determine how successful a company is by looking at statistics.

❀ Martha Stewart has written 13 books. Two of them have made *The New York Times* best-seller list, and one of them (*Martha Stewart's Christmas,* published in 1989) reached number one on that list.

❀ *Martha Stewart's Healthy Quick Cook,* her 13th book, was published in late 1997. Its first printing ran 375,000 copies — the largest ever ordered by her publisher, Clarkson N. Potter.

❀ In its first seven years of publication, the circulation of *Martha Stewart Living* increased by nearly ten times, from 250,000 to 2.3 million.

❀ The *Martha Stewart Living* television show airs in 230 markets, covering 97 percent of the United States.

❀ In June 1996, *Time* magazine named Martha Stewart one of America's 25 Most Influential People.

Martha Stewart first learned about style in her teens and early 20s. To earn extra spending money in high school, and later to help pay her way through prestigious Barnard College in New York City, she began modeling.

Young Martha Kostyra was tall with blonde hair and looked like the classic all-American girl. By her junior year in high school, she had landed modeling assignments at expensive department stores such as Bonwit Teller and Bergdorf's. Eventually Martha starred in a television commercial for Lifebuoy soap. In 1961, *Glamour* magazine named her America's Best Dressed College Girl. She continued her modeling work through college (along with less glamorous jobs, such as cleaning houses), in order to support herself and her new husband, Andrew Stewart, while they finished school. Their only child, a daughter named Alexis, was born in 1965.

After Martha graduated from college, she took a job as a **stockbroker** for the New York City firm of Monness, Williams, and Sidel. In an interview with *Working Woman* magazine, she said she earned about $135,000 per year in that position during the late 1960s and early 1970s. In 1973 and 1974, a **recession**—a period of time when people have less money to spend—hit the country. People stopped investing in **stock,** and Martha's earnings, which were partly based on how much she sold, began to drop. She decided to get out of the stock business.

For the first time in her adult life, Martha didn't have a job. She and Andrew decided to move out of New York and into the countryside of Westport, Connecticut. They found a 19th-century farmhouse and started to repair it.

Their new home sat on Turkey Hill Road, so they decided to name it Turkey Hill Farm. Martha has said that the house was "a wreck" when they bought it. It needed a great deal of work, and the couple did everything themselves, except for electrical wiring. After repairing and

stockbroker

A person who buys and sells shares of businesses, called stock, on behalf of his or her clients.

recession

A period of little economic activity when people typically spend most of their money on things they need, such as food and shelter, rather than on things they want, such as a new car or new clothing.

stock

Shared ownership in a company by many people who buy shares, or portions, of stock, hoping that the company will make a profit.

An attractive young woman, Martha (center) helped pay for her college tuition with modeling assignments.

decorating the house and then adding a lovely garden, the farm grew into a showplace. Martha and Andrew even constructed a coop where Martha could raise her own Araucana chickens, a type of bird from South America that lays beautifully colored eggs.

Eventually Martha Stewart would own six houses, but the public considers Turkey Hill her true home. She launched her first catering business from this site, and its kitchen and gardens have served as the sets for her television shows and books.

No matter how hard she worked to renovate Turkey Hill Farm, Martha still wanted to find a job outside her home. She missed the challenge of the business world. Food, deliciously cooked and beautifully prepared, had always been one of her passions. In the mid 1970s, she and a friend, Norma Collier, started a catering business called the Uncatered Affair. The name is a play on words: People use the phrase "a catered affair" to describe an elegant party, with professionally prepared foods served by waiters. Martha and Norma's business took a slightly different route.

Martha and her husband Andrew worked for years to repair the old farmhouse they purchased in Westport, Connecticut. They called the beautiful home Turkey Hill Farm.

It prepared foods that hosts could serve on their own, so it would appear as if they had actually cooked the food themselves, and that the party was "an uncatered affair."

The business survived for just over one year before the two friends began to have a difficult time working together. Norma Collier reported that Martha frequently criticized her, often in front of clients or students in the cooking classes they taught. Unfortunately, Martha and Norma dissolved their partnership on bad terms, but Martha started another catering company on her own. That business, called Martha Stewart Inc., specialized in larger parties, especially those given by corporations to celebrate special occasions.

Martha and an assistant admire antiques in the kitchen at Turkey Hill Farm in 1988.

Martha Stewart's first book, Entertaining, *was published in 1982, but the book is still a popular source of advice for people who want to throw a fun and unusual party.*

One of these corporate parties boasted a fairy-tale theme, with rooms decorated as magical forests and waitresses dressed as nymphs. One guest at this affair worked as an editor at the Clarkson N. Potter publishing house. The food and decorations impressed him so much that he asked Martha whether she would like to write a book about entertaining. Martha replied that she was very interested in the idea. With the help of writer Elizabeth Hawes, Martha began to put the book together in 1979.

Since publishing Entertaining *in 1982, Martha Stewart has written many more books, and all have been popular with fans across North America.*

In 1982, Clarkson N. Potter published *Entertaining,* a beautiful cookbook, packed with glossy photographs, interesting recipes, and helpful hints for throwing big parties. *Entertaining* was also expensive: The cover price was $35. Some editors wondered whether people would buy a cookbook that cost so much, but it sold extremely well. Readers can still buy it today, along with the 12 other cooking, entertaining, gardening, and wedding-planning books Martha has written.

Over the next decade, *Entertaining* and Martha's other books became extremely popular. Finally Time, Inc. offered

Whenever Martha introduces a new book, she visits bookstores across the country to autograph copies for her fans.

circulation

The number of copies
sold of a magazine
or newspaper.

to form a partnership with her and develop a magazine called *Martha Stewart Living*®. The magazine would include the type of cooking, decorating, craft, and gardening tips found in Martha's books. Martha agreed to a deal through which Time, the publishers of *Time* and *People* magazines, would own *Martha Stewart Living* magazine, but they would pay her a significant salary to produce it.

Time launched the magazine in 1991, and **circulation** for the first year reached about 250,000. Like her books, the magazine contains full-color pages of beautiful photographs. A talented staff writes many of the articles appearing in the magazine, but Martha finds the time to pen a few stories and columns herself. One of the most popular, called *Remembering,* features Martha's memories of special moments in her own life. By 1997, readership of *Martha Stewart Living* had jumped to more than 2.3 million. In addition to its 10 regular issues each year, the magazine publishes four special issues called *Martha Stewart Living Weddings.* These magazines were created to take advantage of the popularity of her book *Weddings,* published in 1988.

Television seemed like the next world for Martha to conquer. In 1993, *Martha Stewart Living* premiered as a half-hour syndicated series that appeared once a week, giving Martha's fans a chance to actually see her at work. The show proved so popular that it now runs six days every week.

In 1997, before her television program went daily, Martha and Time mutually agreed to end their partnership. The reason for this, according to published reports, was

In April 1998, Martha officially opened her new television studio and production facility, located in Westport, Connecticut.

Time's unwillingness to spend the money necessary to expand Martha's operations. Martha apparently wanted more control over her own future as well. She bought her magazine from the company for about $75 million. Since then, Martha actually owns the magazine, rather than merely receiving a salary to produce it for someone else.

With her freedom from Time, Martha started her current company, Martha Stewart Living Omnimedia. The company runs all her business ventures, including the publication of her books, magazines, and newspaper columns and the production of her television show and radio program. It distributes Martha merchandise at Kmart® in the United States and Zellers® in Canada, as well as through the Martha By Mail® catalog. It is also in charge of the official Internet site for Martha fans.

Martha Stewart Living Omnimedia consists of three distinct groups: the publishing group, the television group, and the merchandising group.

Virtual Martha

People who want to learn more about Martha Stewart can access her official Web site, http://www.marthastewart.com. In addition to reading her favorite recipes, learning new crafts, ordering products from the Martha by Mail catalog, and subscribing to her magazine, users can:

❀ Check out Martha Stewart's weekly calendar to see what events she is attending, where she is working, and what at-home projects she has planned for the week ahead.

❀ Read a short biography about Martha and more about the history of her company.

❀ Read questions from readers that Martha has answered concerning her personal life, including where she gets her hair done and what skin products she uses.

❀ Find helpful tips on pet care, decorating, cooking, entertaining, and holiday fun.

❀ Tour the television set of *Martha Stewart Living*.

❀ Web "surfers" can even e-mail a question to Martha!

Living and Learning

Before the publication of *Entertaining,* Martha Stewart had become well known in Connecticut and New York, both for her catering business and for the lifestyle articles she wrote for several popular magazines and newspapers, including *Bon Appetit, The New York Times,* and *Country Living.* She also served as a food editor for *House Beautiful.*

Entertaining made Martha Stewart a star, bringing her ideas about lifestyle to the American public. The book included interesting recipes and beautiful pictures, and it seemed to suggest that anyone could organize an elegant and successful party for as many as 200 guests. Still, some people criticized it. A *New York Times* food editor complained that several recipes simply did not work. Others believed that she had **plagerized** recipes developed by famous chefs.

None of that affected the sales of *Entertaining*. Today more than 600,000 copies have been printed. Martha's publisher quickly asked her to write another volume. She called that book *Martha Stewart's Quick Cook*. By 1997, she had written 13 books. In addition, Clarkson N. Potter has published 10 books under the series title "The Best of Martha Stewart Living." These volumes compile favorite ideas that have appeared in the magazine over the years, including titles such as *Special Occasions* and *How to Decorate*. All Martha's books are sold under the supervision of Martha Stewart Living® Omnimedia.

The company's publishing group also produces *Martha Stewart Living* magazine. Like her books, it brings Martha's ideas about do-it-yourself cooking, gardening, housekeeping, and decorating to people who want to learn new and unusual techniques.

Finally, this group produces the *askMartha* newspaper column and the *askMartha* radio show. The newspaper column appears each week in about 200 newspapers in the United States and Canada. Readers submit their questions about cooking, gardening, and

plagerize

To use another's words and ideas without giving him or her credit.

Today many families enjoy cooking special meals together, often using Martha Stewart's advice to make sure the food turns out just right.

crafts, and Martha and her staff answer them—much the same way that Dear Abby and Ann Landers give advice to their readers. The radio show, which runs for just 90 seconds, is featured each day on 210 stations in the United States.

Reading is a good way to learn new recipes and craft ideas, but some people like watching television even better—especially when they want to attempt difficult creative projects. If someone wants to learn how to cook a gourmet meal, plant a garden, or decorate a house, it can be much easier if he or she can first watch someone else perform the same task, step-by-step.

That's how Martha Stewart made it to television. Although Martha had made guest appearances on other people's programs—and even produced a special or two herself—she got serious about television in 1991. That year she began making weekly appearances on the NBC network's early-morning *Today* program. September of 1993 marked the debut of *Martha Stewart Living,* her own half-hour show. It aired weekly for four years.

Martha observes as a guest explains how to make a special recipe on the set of the Martha Stewart Living *television show.*

In September 1997, Martha struck a deal with the CBS television network to increase her time on the air. Her television show, formerly a once-a-week program, began to run for a half-hour daily. It became so popular that, in early 1999, it began airing for one full hour each weekday. It can be seen in more than 230 regions in the United States and airs on a Canadian cable network as well.

As part of her deal with CBS, Martha also exchanged her weekly appearances on *Today* for similar spots on CBS's *This Morning*. Finally, she occasionally produces prime-time specials for the network. She had completed two by 1998, both Christmas specials. Her guests on these shows are diverse—both Kermit the frog and First Lady Hillary Rodham Clinton have made guest appearances.

Of all these efforts, the *Martha Stewart Living* television show has proved the most popular. By 1998, it had won four Daytime Emmy awards and ranked first in viewership among the eight daily syndicated series that debuted in 1997.

Martha Stewart Living Omnimedia also makes a lot of money through partnerships the company formed with Kmart® and Zellers®. Starting in late 1997, Kmart hired Martha Stewart to develop a new department in all its stores. The department sells sheets, towels, curtains, and paint. It may eventually sell gardening tools as well.

Martha's products, called the Martha Stewart Everyday collection, have become so popular among Kmart customers that the department was expected to make more than $500 million by the end of 1998. One year

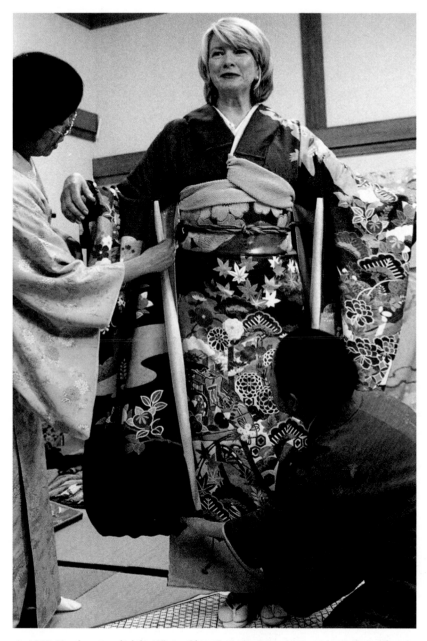

In 1998, Martha attended the Winter Olympics in Nagano, Japan, to contribute lifestyle pieces to the U.S. broadcast of the games. Martha is always ready to try something new, such as doning a traditional Japanese kimono.

later, Martha formed a similar partnership with the
Canadian retailer Zellers, which now markets the
Everyday collection as well.

The Martha Stewart Everyday product line is among
the top-selling brands among shoppers at discount
department stores in the United States. That's good news
for Kmart, a company that has seen its sales decline as

Martha Stewart displays towels from the Everyday collection at Zeller's.

Martha gives step-by-step instructions for completing interesting projects on her television show, and fans can purchase unusual craft products from her catalog.

competitors, such as Wal-Mart®, become more popular. Kmart is counting on Martha Stewart's popularity to draw more customers into its stores. About 70 million people shop at Kmart each year.

Martha Stewart's fans can also buy her goods through the Martha By Mail® catalog. It offers bed and bath sets, books, craft kits, decorating items, household and gardening tools, and many other goods. It was launched in the fall of 1995.

Martha checks out the merchandise at a New York City store.

Martha fans can now use the Internet to learn more about their favorite lifestyle star. Martha Stewart Living Omnimedia launched its Web site in September 1997. Within one year, it attracted about 1.2 million visitors per month. Visitors to the site are greeted with a "welcome" page providing household and lifestyle tips. A few recent ones: to keep iced coffee from getting watery, freeze coffee to make ice cubes; create an interesting centerpiece for the table using herbs instead of flowers.

The Web site offers other features as well. Users may view highlights from upcoming *Martha Stewart Living* television shows. They can read step-by-step instructions for recipes, gardening hints, and craft projects. Fans of the magazine can subscribe to *Martha Stewart Living.* Shoppers can even browse Martha's catalog and purchase products on the Internet.

What's in a Name?

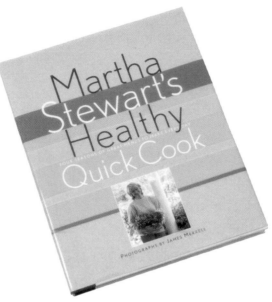

When artists feel proud of their work, they usually sign their name to it. Authors do it, as do painters, composers, and photographers.

Martha Stewart has chosen to place her name on everything her company produces. By doing so, she has turned herself into Martha Stewart Living Omnimedia's most important product. This is both a good and a bad thing. Fans recognize her drive and ambition, and they also see the results of her efforts: She owns six houses around the world, as well as expensive cars. She is also one of the most successful businesswomen in the country.

Fans recognize Martha's creativity and the results of that creativity. She turns old, run-down houses into show-places. She plants lavish gardens. She cooks exotic meals, deliciously cooked and beautifully prepared.

Recently, however, fans have learned about another side of Martha's personality. Several magazine articles, and a biography called *Just Desserts,* have said that she can be difficult to work with—and to work for. She is said to be extremely demanding of her employees, and occasionally she has been critical enough to make them cry. A gardener at Turkey Hill Farm sued Martha and won on the grounds that he had worked hundreds of hours of overtime without pay. Other former employees claim that Martha took credit for their own creativity and ideas.

Not everyone likes Martha. Her obsession with perfection makes it easy to poke fun at her. A **parody** of her books, called *Is Martha Stewart Living?,* has proven popular. So have some skits on television programs such as *Saturday Night Live.* The Internet has numerous anti-Martha Web sites.

Martha's personal life has received negative attention as well. Friends claim that Martha's career was more important to her than her marriage to Andrew Stewart. She may have had little time and energy to devote to her husband, and in 1988, the couple divorced. Martha's acquaintances also claim that motherhood has never been among her priorities.

parody

An imitation of a person; creative work made with the intention of poking fun.

Daughter Alexis, married in 1997, apparently refused to allow her famous mother to help with the wedding plans.

None of this seems to matter to Martha Stewart's millions of fans. Martha has taken advantage of changing times. At the beginning of the 20th century, a woman, her mother, and her grandmother often lived together in the same town. Since fewer women worked outside the home during this era, housekeeping and raising families were their primary occupations. Parents often raised their daughters to be good cooks and learn homemaking skills. If someone needed to know how to make a homemade pie crust, how to

Many people do not live close enough to relatives, such as a mother or grandmother, who can teach them how to make a delicious meal or sew a pretty outfit. Martha Stewart's fans look to her books, magazines, and television program for advice.

After negative attention from the media, Martha Stewart's reputation has faltered, but legions of fans still look to her for advice and creative ideas.

Martha Stewart's publications are one source of information to help gardeners grow healthy plants and design attractive gardens.

plant a vegetable garden, or how to cook a holiday dinner, she could simply ask her mother or grandmother.

At the beginning of the 21st century, family life has changed significantly. Today people often live far from their extended families, so it isn't always easy to ask older relatives for advice. As more and more women enter the workplace, there is also less time to pursue creative projects at home and less time to do housework. Many families still want their homes to look their best.

They want to cultivate gardens full of ripe vegetables for the table and colorful flowers that can be cut and arranged in a vase. Both mothers and fathers want to treat their families to delicious, creative meals. People all over North America turn to Martha Stewart and her books, magazines, and television program for advice on how to run a beautiful, well-organized home.

In June 1998, Martha Stewart hosted a reception for members of the Democratic party. President Clinton was among the guests who enjoyed a special luncheon planned by Martha herself.

Martha Stewart Living Omnimedia earned approximately $200 million in 1998. The amount of money the company makes will probably increase as it expands into new ventures, but the company needs to raise money to help it grow. To do so, Martha Stewart Living Omnimedia may go public, which means it will begin to sell stock in the company.

As of 1999, Martha Stewart Living Omnimedia was a privately held company, meaning that only a small number

Martha takes a break from her hectic schedule to enjoy a backyard barbecue.

Martha Stewart poses with one of her pets, a beautiful Chow Chow.

initial public offering

The first time a company allows the public to buy shares of its stock.

shares

Portions of stock owned by investors in a business.

of individuals or groups own any portion of it. If a company wants or needs to raise money, it may hold an **initial public offering,** which means that it will sell pieces of the company to anyone who has the desire—and the money—to buy them. These pieces of the company are called **shares.** Typically, an initial public offering can bring a lot of cash into a company, cash that can be used for expansion or to bring new ideas to life.

Martha Stewart believes there is still room in the marketplace to expand her company. She regularly uses computer technology to help run her life and her business, and she has suggested that the company may produce an electronic system to help people organize their households. She also hopes to sell even more products to the public, especially some that are developed specifically for the Christmas holiday season.

Only Martha Stewart and her staff know what route the company will travel next. Two things are certain, however. The first is that a large number of Americans have fallen in love with Martha's ideas and unusual products. The second is that Martha sits firmly at the helm of her company: With her drive, ambition, and popularity, she usually gets what she wants.

Team Martha

While Martha Stewart's image and ideas are the company's main product, she doesn't do all the work on her own. A talented staff helps develop new lifestyle ideas and run the organization.

Other than Martha herself, perhaps the most visible member of the team at Martha Stewart Living® Omnimedia is Sharon Patrick. As president of the company, she ranks just below Martha in the corporate hierarchy.

Martha and Sharon have been friends and business partners for several years. Sharon, who holds a master's degree in business administration from Harvard University, helped Martha during the negotiations that helped secure the company's freedom from Time, Inc. She is said to be a smart businessperson. Prior to accepting her present position, Sharon worked for a cable television company called Rainbow Programming Holdings. Reports say that during her three years at the company, she increased its earnings by 50 percent.

While Martha brings her creative ideas to the marketplace, Sharon focuses her energy on making sure those ideas will sell. She has an excellent idea of what products people will buy, and how much they are willing to pay for them. Together Martha and Sharon make a powerful pair, leading the team at Martha Stewart Living Omnimedia.

Important Moments

1941
Martha Kostyra is born in Nutley, New Jersey.

Mid-1950s
Martha begins modeling.

1961
Martha marries Andrew Stewart.

1964
Martha graduates from Barnard College.

1965
Martha and Andrew's only child, Alexis, is born.

Mid-1960s
Martha takes a job as a stockbroker at the firm of Monness, Williams, and Sidel.

1972
Martha and Andrew buy Turkey Hill Farm.

Mid-1970s
Martha and Norma Collier launch a catering business, The Uncatered Affair. Martha then launches her second catering business, Martha Stewart Inc.

Martha writes lifestyle articles for periodicals such as House Beautiful, Bon Appetit, The New York Times, *and* Country Living.

1982
Entertaining, *Martha's first book, is published.*

1991
Martha and Time, Inc. launch Martha Stewart Living *magazine.*

1991
Martha begins appearing weekly on NBC's Today *program.*

1993
Martha Stewart Living debuts as a once-a-week, half-hour show.

1995
The Martha By Mail catalog is launched.

1997
Martha and Time dissolve their relationship.

Martha starts a new company, Martha Stewart Living Omnimedia.

Martha's television program airs daily. She ends her guest appearances on Today a*nd begins to appear weekly on* This Morning.

Martha forges a relationship with Kmart to sell her Everyday line in stores nationwide.

Martha's Web site is launched.

1998
Martha forms an alliance with Zellers department store in Canada to sell her Everyday line.

1999
The Martha Stewart Living *television program expands to a full hour.*

Glossary

chief executive officer (CEO)
The person responsible for managing a company and making decisions that help the company make a profit.

circulation
The number of copies sold of a magazine or newspaper.

initial public offering
The first time a company allows the public to buy shares of its stock.

Internet
A worldwide system of computer networks. The World Wide Web and its Web sites are part of the Internet.

lifestyle
A person's way of life. The food people eat, the way they spend their money, the plants they grow, and the way they decorate their homes, are all part of their lifestyle.

niche
An activity for which a person or thing is best suited.

Omnimedia
Part of the name of Martha Stewart's company. Omni is a Latin word meaning "all," and media refers to different means of communicating information, including newspaper, television, radio, books, and magazines.

parody
An imitation of a person; creative work made with the intention of poking fun.

plagerize   To use another's words or ideas without giving him or her credit.

recession   A period of little economic activity when people typically spend most of their money on things they need, such as food and shelter, rather than on things they want, such as a new car or new clothing.

shares   Portions of stock owned by investors in a business.

stock   Shared ownership in a company by many people who buy shares, or portions, of stock, hoping that the company will make a profit.

stockbroker   A person who buys and sells shares of businesses, called stock, on behalf of his or her clients.

Index

Items in bold print indicate illustration.

Further Information

BOOKS:

Brennan, Georgeanne, et al. *The Children's Kitchen Garden: A Book of Gardening, Cooking, and Learning.* Berkeley, CA: Ten Speed Press, 1997.

Elliot, Marion. *100 Things for Kids to Make and Do.* New York: Smithmark Publishing, 1997.

Karnes, Frances A. et al. *Girls and Young Women Entrepreneurs.* Minneapolis, MN: Free Spirit, 1997.

Meachum, Virginia. *Martha Stewart: Successful Businesswoman.* Springfield, NJ: Enslow Publishers, 1998.

Scott, Emily. *Dinner from Dirt: 10 Meals Kids Can Grow and Cook.* Salt Lake City, UT: Gibbs Smith, 1998.

WEB SITES:

In addition to the official Martha Stewart Web site, (http://www.marthastewart.com), visit other guides to Martha Stewart sites on the Web:
http://www.du.edu/~szerobni
http://www.charlotte.com/special/martha/html/